THE VANDAL

BY HAMISH LINKLATER

★

★

DRAMATISTS
PLAY SERVICE
INC.

THE VANDAL
Copyright © 2013, Hamish Linklater

All Rights Reserved

SPECIAL NOTE

First produced in New York City by
The Flea Theater
Jim Simpson, Artistic Director; Carol Ostrow, Producing Director

For Jack

THE VANDAL was presented by The Flea Theater (Jim Simpson, Artistic Director; Carol Ostrow, Producing Director; Beth Dembrow, Managing Director) in New York City, opening on January 31, 2013. It was directed by Jim Simpson; the set design was by David M. Barber; the lighting design was by Brian Aldous; the costume design was by Claudia Brown; the original music and sound design were by Brandon Wolcott; and the stage manager was Michelle Kelleher. The cast was as follows:

WOMAN .... Deirdre O'Connell
BOY... Noah Robbins
MAN .... Zach Grenier

CHARACTERS

WOMAN

BOY

MAN

THE VANDAL

Scene 1

Night, cold, a bus stop in Kingston. A woman waits. A boy comes up.

BOY. Has it come yet?

WOMAN. No.

BOY. Late. *(Woman nods.)* Always late. *(Woman nods.)* Unless you miss it. Then you're late, you're the one who's late. Not the bus.

WOMAN. Yeah. I guess.

BOY. I guess. I guess if it came, if it weren't late, you wouldn't be here, right? I mean, like, why would you be here if it had come on time? You would be on the bus, and not here, keeping me company. *(Pause.)*

WOMAN. It may have, I was, I was a little late, so it may have already come …

BOY. Then we're in trouble, we are in trouble! It's like 20 minutes till the next one, right?

WOMAN. I think —

BOY. Oh my God, we're gonna freeze! We're gonna have to totally like, huddle together for warmth, just to survive. *(Woman looks at boy.)* Kidding, I'm kidding. *(Pause.)* Where you headed?

WOMAN. Home.

BOY. Where's that? *(Beat.)* Sure gets dark early, huh … You come from the cemetery?

WOMAN. What?

BOY. The cemetery? *(He points off.)* That's where I was. I had a friend who died, about a year ago. I like to visit sometimes after school, say a prayer, check in, y'know, if it's a mess I clean up a little, get rid of the leaves.

WOMAN. Oh.

BOY. Is that where you were?

WOMAN. No. The Hospital. *(She points off in another direction.)*

BOY. Oh right! I think that's hilarious, I always do, that, like, the hospital and the grave yard are right next door, it's like, what genius city planner...?

WOMAN. I know.

BOY. I mean, I guess it's practical, it's like economical, if things don't go well in one place it's a short drive to the next, but still, if you're going to the hospital and you're really sick, which you probably are because you're going to the hospital, it's not very —

WOMAN. Encouraging.

BOY. Ha! Exactly. Or even if you're not sick, if you're like having a baby, you can't get too psyched cuz there's the cemetery as you drive up, you're like, "Yay, New Life! Oooooooo right, we're all gonna die, shoot almost forgot. Thanks, city planner."

WOMAN. *(Pointing off.)* And then there's the liquor store around the corner.

BOY. I know! That's like the one thing the city planner got right, like if you have to go to one or other of the other two places, and you're able to stumble out alive, at least there's the liquor store waiting for you. We're at the center of the triangle. *(Points at the hospital.)* Dying. *(Points at cemetery.)* Dead. *(Points at liquor store.)* Drunk. Are you sick?

WOMAN. What? No, why?

BOY. Is that why you were at the hospital?

WOMAN. No, my friend. I went to see a friend.

BOY. A friend, a-ha. Are you the friend, or do you really have a friend? Like when people say, "I have this friend who likes you," or "I have this friend who had a gay experience, but he's totally straight," or "I have this friend who pretends he's clumsy, but his dad beats the shit out of him," or "I have this friend who's freezing his ass off right now" but it's really you who's the friend —

WOMAN. I have a friend. An actual friend.

BOY. Oh no, I bet you do. Me too. I just told you about like five friends of mine, except the last one, the freezing one, that was me. No, I bet you have lots of friends.

WOMAN. What's that mean?

BOY. You're pretty. You're a little cold, but that might just be the weather. But I think you're probably nice too, when you warm up.

So I bet people want to be friends with you.

WOMAN. Okay. Well. Thank you.

BOY. Hey, would you buy me a beer?

WOMAN. What?

BOY. I was, while we wait, could you buy me a beer, from the liquor store?

WOMAN. Why can't you buy your own? *(Boy looks at her.)* I don't think you can just drink beer outside, on the street.

BOY. Why not?

WOMAN. It's the law.

BOY. I'm the law.

WOMAN. Well then why can't you buy a beer for yourself, Law Man?

BOY. Because the Liquor Man has a bat and he doesn't believe me.

WOMAN. That you're 21?

BOY. That I'm The Law.

WOMAN. *(Laughs.)* How old are you?

BOY. How old are you?

WOMAN. Rude.

BOY. Why? Why is it polite to ask young people their age? Why is that gracious and charming?

WOMAN. You look 17.

BOY. You look old enough to be my sexy aunt.

WOMAN. How old's your sexy aunt?

BOY. I don't have one — yet.

WOMAN. If you are 17, I'm old enough to be your mother.

BOY. My mother's dead. She's up there too. That's not who I was visiting just now, that was my friend.

WOMAN. I'm sorry.

BOY. It's ok, it's not bad, she died before I was born. Or like, she had died, and they had to do an emergency c-section to save me, but so, I never knew her. It's not so bad missing someone you never knew, though, y'know what I mean? It's not so bad.

WOMAN. Still, I'm very sorry.

BOY. So, will you buy me a beer? I'll pay.

WOMAN. I don't think so.

BOY. You're not conservative, are you?

WOMAN. What do you mean, politically?

BOY. Temperamentally. Not "a conservative," my dad's "a conservative," I just meant "conservative."

WOMAN. Because I wouldn't buy a kid alcohol? If that's ... then, yeah, I guess I'm like your dad on that one.

BOY. You don't wanna be like my dad.

WOMAN. Oh no?

BOY. What about when you were younger? I bet you were more liberal.

WOMAN. When I was younger? I don't remember.

BOY. Because you were drunk all the time?

WOMAN. Sure. People were much nicer than me in my day. They'd buy beer for you at the bus stop no problem.

BOY. I miss the old days.

WOMAN. You're funny.

BOY. We both are.

WOMAN. I'm not. I'm not.

BOY. I bet you're hilarious when you get your drink on.

WOMAN. Well that's not happening tonight, so I guess we'll just have to live in the ... I can't remember —

BOY. Why not tonight? Because of your friend? *(Pause.)* I had a teacher just like you.

WOMAN. Oh, now I'm your teacher, I thought I was your sexy aunt.

BOY. I told you, I don't have an aunt. But I had a teacher, Mrs. Bluh — Wait, you might know her. Do you live in the area?

WOMAN. I do. I live here.

BOY. Why don't you have a car?

WOMAN. It's at the mechanic.

BOY. You can't afford it?

WOMAN. It's at the mechanic.

BOY. You had to sell it?

WOMAN. It's at the mechanic.

BOY. When'll it be ready?

WOMAN. Soon.

BOY. Is that why you can't afford to buy me beer? I told you, I'll pay —

WOMAN. You had a sexy teacher?

BOY. I didn't say that she was sexy, I said you reminded me of her.

WOMAN. Oh.

BOY. She had sex with a senior at my school, Matt Hoop — wait you might know him too.

WOMAN. I don't, I mean why would I —

BOY. He killed himself. It was in the paper.

WOMAN. If it was in the paper, why can't you say their names?

BOY. You might not have bought the paper that day; they've gotten expensive, newspapers. She got pregnant, Mrs. Bl — and she wanted to keep it because she was — how old are you again? Doesn't matter. She was much older than you and she didn't think there was any way, I mean there probably wasn't, this was her shot, it wasn't that she was ugly, she had dated this French guy, I don't know his real name, we called him Pierre, and they had been together for like ten years, he didn't believe in marriage, maybe his father had fucked around, like Mitterrand, so he didn't believe in it —

WOMAN. How do you know?

BOY. My friend Tim Ross' mom was talking, or drinking wine and guessing, and Pierre was either against having kids because of coming from a broken home, or just sterile, and then Mrs. Bl — , the teacher, when she turned 40, he left her, just went back to France, or met someone else, Tim Ross' mom didn't know for sure, anyway Pierre was suddenly gone and the teacher was suddenly 40 and crying all the time in class which was just embarrassing for the kids, it was so pathetic, and as a result we had like, as a class, the lowest AP French scores in the county —

WOMAN. She taught —

BOY. French, so it was like torture, every word she said was part of a conversation with Pierre she would never have again, just *bleh, bleh, bleh,* blub, blub, blub all the time, I even went to the principal to get her fired, or sent on sabbatical till she got her shit together, not because I loved French so much, though I am pretty good at it, *"On n'apprend pas aux vieux singes à faire des grimaces,"* (that's a French proverb), but no, I wanted her fired because it was just so disgusting, the sob fest, and then, so, when she got pregnant and it was Matt Hoop — who was only in AP French because his dad was an undertaker and had like a chain of funeral homes, started with nothing but a shovel and a pair of black pants, put himself through Wesleyan, he was determined Matt would go to Wesleyan too, (but then Matt was a legacy so it shouldn't have been that hard, maybe he just needed an AP attended on his admissions.) anyway Matt got like straight F's, he was always zonked out in the back of class, Zoloft probably, all in black like his dad, but ironically, I think, to piss his dad off, but so that's why — I mean I thought it even

11

before I heard Tim Ross' mom say it — why Mrs. Bl — chose Matt to get pregnant by, because Matt would never learn to say shit in French, not *merde*. But then, when she told him she was keeping it? Matt killed himself in that crazy way.

WOMAN. What way?

BOY. It was on TV. You don't even own a TV?

WOMAN. I own a TV, I just don't remember —

BOY. Or did you have to sell it with the car?

WOMAN. I just don't remember this story —

BOY. Self-entombment.

WOMAN. What?

BOY. That's what he died by: self-entombment.

WOMAN. What do you mean?

BOY. He buried himself alive. *(Silence.)*

WOMAN. How?

BOY. It was kinda genius. There was a funeral that his dad was handling and he just swapped himself for the guy who was being buried. It was a closed-casket deal, the dead guy, the already-dead guy, Mr. Quinn I think, had died of some horrible like wasting disease, like Ebola of the head, and Matt's dad was like, "I can spruce him up and you can have the open casket but it'll cost you an arm and a leg to fix his face", and the Quinn family, they were Catholic and poor, not unrelatedly, and Mrs. Quinn, formerly Fleischer, was still kinda young so maybe she wanted to save a little heading into the second chapter of her life, not Tim Ross' mom's favorite, Mrs. Quinn nee Fleischer, so they went closed casket, but then when Mr. Quinn, or maybe it was O'Keefe, anyway when he was found in the woods by the road looking even more wasted, half-eaten by woodlen creatures and all, everyone wondered who they had just buried, cause the coffin definitely had a body in it, it was heavy. Imagine it, Matt must've had to lay so still … So when they dug up the casket it was too late of course, he'd suffocated, or just, I don't know what kills you in self-entombment, dehydration maybe, but at some point he had changed his mind because it was a mess in there, he'd torn at the insides of the lid, all the lining, the stuffing was torn out, and it stank of course because you lose control of your functions when you die, you literally lose your shit, but it was also supposed to be beautiful with him all covered in ripped-out white stuffing — like he was laying in a cloud, or a bath of angel feathers.

WOMAN. Was that who you were visiting?

BOY. What? No, I didn't really like Matt, I know tons of people who have died. This is Kingston. Just from my high school Becky Morse took heroin before going to the dentist and OD'ed on the Novocain, Marshall Swee's older brother died in Afghanistan, Kellen Hertz died of MS or ALS, I always get them confused; my friend who I was visiting? A year ago he and three other kids were in a car that just wrecked on the way to school cuz it was icy and the tires were a little bald and they all died, just from a slippery road.

WOMAN. Jesus.

BOY. What? It happens all the time, everywhere. What would be really crazy is if people stopped dying, everywhere. That would be a story for the paper. So anyway, Mrs. Bl — had to quit, but she had her daughter seven months later, it had a cleft pallet or something, it wasn't perfect, but it was something you could fix, and she never cried again.

WOMAN. That's who I remind you of?

BOY. Yeah.

WOMAN. Maybe you should have stuck with the sexy aunt line if you wanted a beer.

BOY. I just meant you both seem like women who see life, that it's short, and like, much easier to waste than use. And when you see a chance, y'know, to have sex with some AP French burn-out so you can have a life with a baby instead of one without, or when you see a chance to buy a funny kid a beer so that your freezing wait for a bus is noisy and entertaining instead of quiet and boring, you both choose life! Life! Life! Rah, rah, rah! *(Woman looks for the bus. It isn't coming. She laughs, opens her purse.)* Oh no. I got it. I insist. Here, pay with this. *(He gives her a $20.)*

WOMAN. What do you want?

BOY. Just Bud.

WOMAN. Bud. Just, what? One or —

BOY. They come in six; we can share.

WOMAN. Okay. We'll see. *(Woman takes the $20, goes off toward liquor store. Boy does something magical, like a front flip off the bench. The sound of the bus, he looks for her, it goes black as the bus pulls in front of him.)*

Scene 2

Liquor store. Man behind counter. Woman puts six-pack of Bud down. Pause.

MAN. That it?
WOMAN. Yep.
MAN. Just the Budweiser?
WOMAN. Uhuh.
MAN. No chips or cigarettes or —
WOMAN. I don't smoke.
MAN. So … just the Budweiser?
WOMAN. Yes. *(Pause.)*
MAN. Okay.
WOMAN. Is that a problem?
MAN. You just don't strike me as a Budweiser drinker.
WOMAN. Oh no?
MAN. Not really.
WOMAN. What do I strike you as?
MAN. More of a wine drinker maybe.
WOMAN. That's —
MAN. I'm not being sexist. If I thought you were French I'd think you drink wine too. That doesn't mean I think all French people are women. Just playing the percentages. Because I sell a fair amount of Budweiser, but very rarely to middle-aged, nonsmoking women … But you're right, it's wrong, profiling people. *(Woman laughs.)* What?
WOMAN. Nothing. French. Private joke. Nothing.
MAN. You sure you don't want some chips. Lotta beer on an empty stomach.
WOMAN. I don't want chips.
MAN. You have food already? Maybe a pizza in the car?
WOMAN. That's right. *(Man looks out the window.)* I parked round the corner.
MAN. That's weird. We got parking out front.
WOMAN. My spot's fine.

14

MAN. It's a cold night.

WOMAN. My coat's very warm.

MAN. Doesn't look it.

WOMAN. It is.

MAN. Not a great neighborhood. You got pepper spray?

WOMAN. I do.

MAN. I got a bat.

WOMAN. *(Beat.)* That's good.

MAN. You have to defend yourself. Against lawlessness. Maybe I should walk you to your car.

WOMAN. I'm fine. I'll be fine.

MAN. So just the six Budweisers?

WOMAN. You know what, I will get some chips. I'm low on chips. Thank you, thank you for the suggestion. *(Woman grabs some chips.)*

MAN. He doesn't like Sun Chips. He likes Cool Ranch Doritos.

WOMAN. Who?

MAN. My son. Robert. He likes Cool Ranch Doritos. If you're gonna get chips too.

WOMAN. I don't know who you're talking about.

MAN. You shouldn't buy beer for minors. It's illegal.

WOMAN. Why would you think —

MAN. You're buying Budweiser.

WOMAN. It's a popular beer.

MAN. It's his favorite.

WOMAN. It's many people's favorite. Hence its popularity.

MAN. "Hence." Oooooo. *(Silence.)* First Friday of the month. Little shit always sends someone in to buy him Budweiser first Friday of the month. Mostly they're homeless though. Not that I'm profiling you as not homeless. Just, they're usually the type of person that buys a kid a beer because they need one for themselves. And they're usually not women, or I should say attractive women. So, how's he doing? Did he tell you my wife is dead? To get you to come in here? Little shit.

WOMAN. I never met your son.

MAN. He says stuff like that to manipulate a situation to his advantage. Which is fine, no one wants to manipulate a situation to their disadvantage.

WOMAN. You don't get a lot of people buying Budweiser on a Friday night?

MAN. Oh, I'm not the most popular small business in Kingston.

WOMAN. Can't imagine why; are you gonna let me pay for this?

MAN. $12.49. *(Woman lays down the $20.)* Out of twenty. Without going over. Y'know that's his allowance money? Y'know that twenty came out of this till? I know it's not much of an allowance. I know, I'm not much for inflation. But once a month some derelict comes in here, buys Budweiser and whatever else without going over twenty, and I know who it is they're buying it for. Where is he? By the bus stop?

WOMAN. I wouldn't know.

MAN. You can tell me. It's not like I'm gonna run out there and try to catch him. Give him a beating for making a pretty lady buy him beer.

WOMAN. You're not gonna do that?

MAN. He's too fast for me. Time I reach the corner Robert's gone, every time. It's like I set off his spidey sense. How did he seem to you?

WOMAN. I don't know your son.

MAN. I could call the police if you're contributing to the corruption of a minor.

WOMAN. I'll take a half-pint of Jim Beam, and a pack of Camels. Ultra light. Am I over twenty dollars now? Do I fit the profile of a lady Budweiser drinker now?

MAN. I thought you didn't smoke.

WOMAN. I used to, but I quit, and now I'd like to start again.

MAN. They'll kill you.

WOMAN. What won't?

MAN. Oooo lala.

WOMAN. Oui, Oui.

MAN. $26.63. *(Woman pulls a few singles out of her purse, fishes around, then puts the $20 back and hands him a credit card, he glances at it.)* Can I see some ID?

WOMAN. ID?

MAN. You're purchasing alcohol.

WOMAN. I'm over 21.

MAN. I'm sure you are. But we card anyone under 35.

WOMAN. I'm over 35.

MAN. You don't look it to me.

WOMAN. Are you flirting?

MAN. Would you like me to?

WOMAN. Now you are.

MAN. Now I am.

WOMAN. What would your wife think?

MAN. We're divorced, Libby lives in Long Island with her new family, they play tennis. She'll never know I was flirting.

WOMAN. Okay.

MAN. So can I see some ID?

WOMAN. Is this still flirting, or just annoying?

MAN. Probably annoying. But still store policy.

WOMAN. Who makes the policy?

MAN. Me. It's my store. I'm the Liquor Man.

WOMAN. Fine. *(She fishes through her bag again, hands over ID.)*

MAN. Nice to meet you Margaret Cotter. I'm Dan.

WOMAN. Okay.

MAN. Do you go by Peggy or Maggie?

WOMAN. I don't.

MAN. You are over 21 and 35. I wouldn't believe it if I didn't have certified proof from the State of New York.

WOMAN. Thank God we're back to flirting.

MAN. But then who's Mary Willits? *(He holds up the credit card.)* I mean, I know who she is, she works at the hospital. Beautiful. Like a stunner, and so nice. And I guess there may be two Mary Willits', but according to your driver's license it looks like you're not one of them.

WOMAN. *(Beat.)* Mary's a friend.

MAN. Oh?

WOMAN. She loaned me her card.

MAN. She loaned you her credit card?

WOMAN. Yes.

MAN. You don't have your own credit card?

WOMAN. It's just, it's for emergencies.

MAN. Why would Mary loan you her credit card for emergencies?

WOMAN. She's my friend, and I've had a hard time, financially, and she was worried for me, if I ever got in a tight spot, she wanted me to have a fall-back.

MAN. That's a good friend.

WOMAN. She is.

MAN. Did you go to school together?

WOMAN. No.

MAN. Because you're a little older than she is —

WOMAN. I know her from the hospital —

MAN. Do you work together?

WOMAN. Forget it, I'm leaving.

MAN. I'll call the police.

WOMAN. For a borrowed credit card?

MAN. Then I'll call Mary.

WOMAN. Do you have her number?

MAN. I have a phone book. *(Man pulls out a phone book, starts flipping through.)*

WOMAN. My husband died.

MAN. My wife died too, according to my son.

WOMAN. You're saying my husband didn't die?

MAN. I'm saying it looks like bullshit is catching.

WOMAN. You're saying I'd make something like that up?

MAN. I'm saying I think my son's out there at that bus stop.

WOMAN. *(Furious, pulls a picture from wallet.)* This is my husband Paul Cotter, he fucking died 6 months ago of fucking cancer at Benedictine fucking Hospital, right up on that fucking hill there, and his nurse was Mary Willits! *(Man stops flipping through phone book, looks at picture.)*

MAN. I'm sorry.

WOMAN. Did you kill him?

MAN. No.

WOMAN. Then save your sorries, and let me have my ID and fucking credit card back.

MAN. You're young.

WOMAN. Oh now I'm young again, that's great.

MAN. For a widow.

WOMAN. That has to be the worst compliment ever given.

MAN. I wasn't trying —

WOMAN. Then give me my cards back.

MAN. You don't want the Budweiser?

WOMAN. No.

MAN. My son will be disappointed.

WOMAN. Your son, who I never met, can go fuck himself for all I care. *(Beat. Woman holds her hand out for cards, man doesn't give them.)*

MAN. Okay, miss. I'll give you back your ID, and I'll even give you back Mary's card, but I'm gonna call her first. I have to, that's only fair —

WOMAN. I can't believe —

MAN. And I'm having trouble believing, "hence" our little impasse here.

WOMAN. You need a better explanation than —

MAN. Yeah.

WOMAN. Than a friend helping a friend in need?

MAN. No sure, that's a friend indeed. I just think it's a little far-fetched, nurses handing out their credit cards —

WOMAN. *(More furious.)* Okay, you look. Look me in the eyes, you asshole. My husband got diagnosed with stage 4 testicular cancer. He was forty-five years old. They gave him six months to live. It took him three years to die. And Mary was his nurse, at his bedside, that whole time.

MAN. And that's how you became friends?

WOMAN. That's right. She's my friend, our friend, became our friend — because we lost everything —

MAN. You lost everything —

WOMAN. Everything, my husband quit his job when they told him and I did too, so we could spend those last months —

MAN. Okay.

WOMAN. But then he didn't die, and she was there for all of it, the chemo, the radiation, for the loans, the second mortgages, she was there for us losing everything, and she was great!

MAN. She is great.

WOMAN. I know.

MAN. A real angel.

WOMAN. I know. I know. So sympathetic, so beautiful. Everybody loves Mary.

MAN. Well it's good you had that time.

WOMAN. You think?

MAN. To say goodbye, say what you needed to —

WOMAN. *(Enraged.)* Oh my God, people say that! — Y'know what time's good for? Nothing. A heart attack's better, a car crash, a bolt from the blue- you wanna tell me it's better to watch my husband die for three years —

MAN. No —

WOMAN. Getting a little hope up maybe, and then getting punched in the gut, over and over, that's better? If he's gonna die, fucking kill him already! Here's how you say goodbye for three years, "Goooooooooooooooooooooooooooooooodbyyyyyyyyyyyyyyyyyyyyye,

19

IIIIIIIII looooooooooooooooooove yooooooooooooooooou."

MAN. Okay.

WOMAN. *(More enraged.)* And you wanna know why? Why he didn't die? I'll tell you why. Mary fucking Willits, that Angel. We'd joke the only reason he wouldn't kick off was her, that he'd fallen for her — 'cuz like you said, she was such a ray of sunshine, you know, washing him, all angelic, I mean we'd laugh about it, Paul and I, it was ridiculous, him staying alive so he could just keep going in to see her, gorgeous Mary Willits, keep getting cared for by this heavenly. And then, as if to prove the joke, and it's hilarious, after three years Mary got married to this doctor, Dr. Stevenson, and he, my husband Paul, he took a turn that was bad, and he finally did die, and I don't even think she really loved the doctor, Dr. Stevenson, I mean he was successful, but nothing to look at, or talk to. I think she just knew, I think she knew, after they took the car away, she knew; so she married this guy she didn't love so my husband could die, and I could, you know, move on.

MAN. And that's why she loaned you her credit card?

WOMAN. It's only for emergencies.

MAN. Like buying Budweiser for my son?

WOMAN. I don't know anything about your son. *(Man flips through phone book.)*

MAN. Willow, Wilmot, Winston, oops, wrong way — Williams, Williams, Williams, there must be like thirty Williams, here we go — *(Man dials phone.)*

WOMAN. Fine. I took it. Everything else is true. *(It rings.)* We lost everything, I don't know if he loved her or not, but he died, she hugged me, said how sorry she was, and I took her credit card. *(It rings.)*

MAN. For emergencies?

WOMAN. For revenge. *(It rings.)*

MAN. How does my son look? Is he Okay? *(From the phone: "hello?")*

WOMAN. Yes. *(Man hangs up. He looks at the credit card.)*

MAN. Does it still work?

WOMAN. Yes.

MAN. Do you use it much?

WOMAN. Groceries, twice a month.

MAN. Nobody cards anymore. Why hasn't she cancelled it?

WOMAN. Because she knows what it's being used for. Because

she knows what she did.

MAN. Because she's an angel. *(Man runs the card. They wait. It goes through.)* It worked. Oh, I should have asked: Any cash back?

WOMAN. No, no thank you.

MAN. Wait. *(Man replaces the Sun Chips with Cool Ranch Doritos.)* Just take these, for Robert, as a trade. Okay? Take these, as your gift to me. *(She does and goes.)*

Scene 3

Bus stop, still cold. Boy there, woman returns with bag.

BOY. How'd it go in there?

WOMAN. Easy peasy. *(Woman hands him bag.)*

BOY. Cool Ranch! My favorite, how'd you know?

WOMAN. Lucky guess.

BOY. You want a Bud?

WOMAN. I want the bottle. *(Woman drinks Jim Beam, boy Bud.)*

BOY. You were gone a long time.

WOMAN. I had a problem with my card.

BOY. You paid?

WOMAN. My treat. *(She returns $20.)*

BOY. Why'd you pay?

WOMAN. Because I did.

BOY. Did something happen?

WOMAN. Just drop it, okay? Or change it, it's just, enough. Enough. Okay?

BOY. Okay. *(He bites a chip.)* You know what I like with Cool Ranch, any Dorito really, as opposed to like a Sun Chip? Or a, I don't know, regular tortilla chip? The flavor dust that gets stuck to your fingers when you bite your chip. See? With Cool Ranch it's like, a blue and gold flavor dust. It's not really the color of ranch dressing. Maybe it's a metaphor: "Cool Ranch." But then look at this: so like, you lick it off, the flavor dust. *(He licks his fingers.)* Voila. But then when you go for the next chip, your fingers are like wet and sticky, so more flavor dust sticks to your fingers, so you lick 'em

21

again, and your fingers get wetter and stickier, so there's gonna be more flavor dust, there's gonna be more licking, and eventually it'll just like coat your fingers, your tongue and lips get all coated too, and who knows eventually if the licking is actually cleaning your fingers, or just shellacking on more layers of pasty flavor dust. It's just like this passing back and forth of smoosh that's losing flavor. It's just this cleaning which isn't even tasting anymore, this cleaning that's only making a bigger mess. It's a negative feedback cycle. And the chip, the start of the whole thing, is like beside the point.

WOMAN. Huh.

BOY. Do you think that's a metaphor?

WOMAN. I'm not sure I'm following.

BOY. Is, like, the chip our Life, the flavor dust our dreams, the fingers reality, they moosh together, and then your mouth is like death?

WOMAN. I'm definitely not —

BOY. Or maybe the chip is your heart, the flavor dust is love, the fingers are heartbreak, and then time just gobbles them up?

WOMAN. What if you just let me drink?

BOY. Wait, no, what if the chip is the soul, the flavor dust is magic, the fingers what you do with your soul, and the mouth Deep Space ... or Oblivion, or whatever that massive thing is which doesn't even know the world exists or we exist or that existence exists, that Vastness which is deafeningly neutral, neither good nor bad, just there, just true, just bigger than thoughts can think, and eyes can see, and mouths can say, and when you think about God, Who no one should really think about, look what happened to Job who was a good guy, and always tried to be good, and God said, "You think you know me? You think you know what I want?" And then he bent Job over and fucked him so hard Job was like, "Okay! I get it, I get it," and God was like, "What? What do you get?" and Job was like, "I get that I don't get it, I won't get it, I can't get it, I get that there is nothing to get, there is only God, and He can fuck you up the ass whenever he wants to!" and God came in Job and blew out Job's brains and humankind has never thought of God, or conceived of the enormity of God since, because the part of our brains that could was blown away that day; that God, the real God, who we don't dare know the omniscience of, the omnipotence of, the plan, the rules of, that God, if He does exist, is only a blue flavor dust speck in the mouth of the True Vastness. We do not matter.

More likely we are anti-matter. More likely it's not a metaphor. Most likely it's just a Cool Ranch Dorito.

WOMAN. You really do like those chips.

BOY. Don't get me started on Bud.

WOMAN. I won't.

BOY. I'll give you a hint. Bud's the counter-argument to Doritos.

WOMAN. The counter-argument.

BOY. The yang to the ying.

WOMAN. The vice to the versa?

BOY. Bud says there is only you. And everything else — time, space, God, blah, blah — everyone else — the drunk, dying, dead, blah, blah — exist inside you, if they exist at all, which is up to you, because only you know, and only you matter. You are the Vastness.

WOMAN. How does it say that?

BOY. Taste it. *(Woman puts down her bottle, opens a Bud, sips it, slugs it.)*

WOMAN. Gotcha.

BOY. Good, right?

WOMAN. Now gimme a Dorito so I can regain some perspective. No, you're right. I like mattering. Mattering, nattering about mattering. Wait. Who am I thinking of? Who's the girl? The one from the book, or the movie, with the blonde hair?

BOY. Does she have a blue dress?

WOMAN. Yes.

BOY. Is there a cat?

WOMAN. Yes.

BOY. And a tea party?

WOMAN. Yes!

BOY. I don't know.

WOMAN. Fuck you, tell me you brat, what's her name?

BOY. I'll give you a hint: she has a Restaurant.

WOMAN. What?

BOY. And Gertrude Stein loved her.

WOMAN. Shut the fuck up and tell me who I'm thinking of!

BOY. She doesn't live here anymore —

WOMAN. Jesus are you a smartass! What school do you go to?

BOY. Kingston High.

WOMAN. Bullshit.

BOY. Bull true.

WOMAN. I went to Kingston High! We didn't have AP French

and AP Metaphor and AP Smartass at Kingston fucking High.

BOY. Maybe they introduced them in the 2000s. Or the '80s?

WOMAN. Smartass!

BOY. Intelligence is 20% education, 20% environment, and 60% hereditary.

WOMAN. So now you're taking shots at my parents?

BOY. I made that up.

WOMAN. So it's a shot at me?

BOY. It's a shot in the dark you dove in front of.

WOMAN. No wonder your father beats you. *(Silence.)*

BOY. He said he was my father?

WOMAN. Oh come on.

BOY. He knew I sent you?

WOMAN. Based on my purchases, he interpolated.

BOY. Why would you think he beat me?

WOMAN. He said he had a bat, and you said you had a clumsy friend, and I extrapolated.

BOY. My friend is Kevin Dumphy, I am not the friend.

WOMAN. And he's not your father.

BOY. He's my dad, and he never touched me, and you should believe me.

WOMAN. He also said you have problems with the truth.

BOY. He has problems with the truth.

WOMAN. He also said your mother was alive. I don't care, he said it. It's just that's pretty messed up. I mean of all the things you've made up tonight, that's the messed-uppedest. I don't care. I like it, the talk. But if I was your mother I'd be pretty hurt knowing that my son was walking around saying I'm dead when I'm actually just playing tennis in Long Island with my new family because my old one consisted of an abusive husband and a pathologically lying son. I'd be pretty hurt.

BOY. My father never touched me.

WOMAN. Okay.

BOY. He shouts sometimes. His wife died. The mother of his child died, so he shouts. That's allowed.

WOMAN. Okay.

BOY. Because that's not fair, losing your partner.

WOMAN. I know.

BOY. You don't know anything, you think you do, but unless you're me, or my dad, instead of you, you don't actually know anything about what we've been through.

WOMAN. If you say so.

BOY. You don't because you're you, and I'm me, and Dad's Dad, and what happened to us only happened to us the way it happened to us.

WOMAN. No two snowflakes are the same.

BOY. You don't know.

WOMAN. Eskimos have a thousand words for snow.

BOY. What are you talking about?

WOMAN. If all the snowflakes in the world got together and made the world's biggest snowball and the Eskimos called it *Germuchnik*, and *Tinkatink*, and *Spooldybooldy* and a thousand other names and the snowball went to hell it would still melt, so —

BOY. I don't know —

WOMAN. I'm saying I don't care, I'm saying looks like snow, I'm saying where's the bus.

BOY. She died giving birth to me.

WOMAN. Your dad says different.

BOY. Why won't you believe me?

WOMAN. I don't not believe you.

BOY. But you believe my dad?

WOMAN. I don't not believe —

BOY. He needs help. *(Boy cries.)*

WOMAN. Oh no. Oh no, sssssshhhhhh. You're gonna get, all your tears and snot are gonna freeze to your face, ssssssshhhh. This is a mess, what a mess.

BOY. He's lying.

WOMAN. Oh gosh, what do you want me to say?

BOY. Say he's lying.

WOMAN. Oh sweetheart, everyone lies.

BOY. No they don't.

WOMAN. Of course they do, come on, you've got to, it's expected, it's common courtesy. Hey, I lied to you earlier.

BOY. When?

WOMAN. When I said I had a friend, at the hospital.

BOY. You were the friend?

WOMAN. You guessed it.

BOY. What's wrong with you?

WOMAN. Nothing, it was just a check-up.

BOY. Then why'd you lie?

WOMAN. Because it wasn't your business and it was nicer than saying "fuck off."

25

BOY. When was the last time you went to the doctor?

WOMAN. Fuck off.

BOY. You have to be vigilant, at your age.

WOMAN. Other things came up.

BOY. Why haven't you gone, do you have a death wish? *(Beat.)* It's okay, if you do, I used to want to die.

WOMAN. No, sweetheart.

BOY. *(Still sniffly.)* Oh, my demographic's suicide rate is surreal. What with the hormones, you get zits and erections and suicidally depressed all the time, and you feel like nobody loves you, which with my mom is true since she never met me, I said that already — but there you are just going around like this, I don't know, this pimply, boner-fest, suicide bomb.

WOMAN. But you don't want to die now.

BOY. Well, let's just say mostly I think I'd be happier to be alive than dead.

WOMAN. You know your mother loved you.

BOY. Oh yeah?

WOMAN. Of course she did.

BOY. When? When I was in utero?

WOMAN. Sure.

BOY. How do you know?

WOMAN. Because she did.

BOY. Did you know her? Did you talk to her when she was pregnant with me? Were you her friend?

WOMAN. No.

BOY. I'm gonna go. *(Angry, he starts to leave.)*

WOMAN. What about the bus?

BOY. I'm gonna walk.

WOMAN. It's freezing.

BOY. I don't care.

WOMAN. How far's your house?

BOY. I'm not going home.

WOMAN. Wait, come on, what if I said I was your mother's friend? Would you believe me then?

BOY. I wouldn't believe you.

WOMAN. No, come on, what if I said, when your mom was pregnant, I was her friend, and she said she loved you, and she said she was so excited to meet you, and she couldn't wait?

BOY. *(Beat.)* What else?

26

WOMAN. What else? She said, she said she couldn't wait, and she, she was so excited to have a son, and she wanted you to be a baseball player so your dad's bat would go to good use.

BOY. Uh-huh.

WOMAN. It's true, she said you were her little blessing and and you were gonna bring purpose to her life —

BOY. She wasn't happy?

WOMAN. No, she was. But your Dad, he could be a little stoic, a little strong silenty. But you, you were gonna be a talker. She was gonna see to that, read to you, get cd's of musicals, she was always listening to — what's the name of a musical?

BOY. *My Fair Lady*?

WOMAN. I don't know that one: *Mary Poppins*. She'd put the speaker right up against her belly, so when you came out you'd be all, "superfragalistic" and no one would be able to get a word in edgewise.

BOY. How did you guys meet?

WOMAN. We went to school together.

BOY. She didn't go to Kingston High. She was from Schenectady.

WOMAN. Which is where we went to middle school together. Before my parents moved here. Did she ever tell you the name of her middle school?

BOY. No.

WOMAN. St. Mary's Middle School, Schenectady, New York. We were thick as thieves. I was a bridesmaid at your parents wedding, she made me wear the ugliest dress, etcetera. So yeah, I was with her when she was pregnant, which is how I know she loved you, her little baby, her Robert. *(Pause.)*

BOY. Did my dad tell you my name? In the store?

WOMAN. He didn't have to, I'm one of Libby's oldest friends. *(Pause.)*

BOY. Can I ask you another question? You don't have to tell me the truth.

WOMAN. Sure.

BOY. Are you my mother?

WOMAN. What?

BOY. Are you the friend? Again?

WOMAN. Ummm.

BOY. Did you somehow survive giving birth to me, have you come back from the dead? Are you her? *(Pause.)*

WOMAN. What if I was?

BOY. How did you do it?

WOMAN. *(Gradually.)* Well, okay … What if that night, after you were delivered and sent home with your dad, okay what if I suddenly came to? What if they had given me this powerful sedative while I was giving birth, lexi-something, and I flat-lined. But Dr. Stevenson, my OB/GYN, he used those paddle things and he brought me back to life. And what if when I came to I had amnesia — from the drugs and the paddles and shock. And what if Dr. Stevenson had always been a little in love with me, since Schenectady even, and when he discovered I had amnesia and couldn't remember you or your dad, he told me that he was my husband. That a new job had opened up in Long Island and we would have to be moving as soon as I was feeling better from my appendectomy. So we moved, and had a family, a family of tennis players. But it wasn't my fault, or anyone's really.

BOY. And what are you doing here now?

WOMAN. *(Beat.)* Well the other day, in Long Island, we were playing doubles, and your half-sister, Helen, she hit a lob, and I went back and your half-brother, Troy, he came forward, and Troy's so über-competitive, he jump-slammed his return, and whacked me in the head with his racket. I got concussed, but it shook free this memory, this memory of a little boy, with a little blue hat, who smelt like me and paradise combined, a baby named Robert who I loved more than my new children and who I had to find at all costs, who I had to put my arm around, *(She does this.)* who I had to tell: Your mother is here. She loves you. She never meant to leave you. And now she's here.

BOY. I love you too.

WOMAN. I know. *(Pause.)*

BOY. Are you really her? *(The bus comes, the stage goes black. The bus drives off, the stage is illuminated, Woman and Boy are still there.)*

WOMAN. I'm not your mother.

BOY. Who are you?

WOMAN. Margaret Cotter.

BOY. We're not related?

WOMAN. We're strangers.

BOY. I don't believe you.

WOMAN. It's true.

BOY. You've never had children?

WOMAN. Never.

BOY. You weren't my mother's friend?

WOMAN. I never met your mother.

BOY. How'd you know how to make all that up?

WOMAN. Maybe I do know something about something.

BOY. Let me see your stomach.

WOMAN. What?

BOY. I wanna see if you have a c-section scar.

WOMAN. I don't have, I'm not showing you my stomach.

BOY. Please.

WOMAN. What are you talking about?

BOY. Please!

WOMAN. It's freezing!

BOY. I knew it, I knew you were her!

WOMAN. Fine. There! *(She opens her coat and pulls up her shirt and down the front of her pants.)* There, see my stupid, horrible, scarless, stomach. *(He looks.)*

BOY. What's that?

WOMAN. What?

BOY. That line?

WOMAN. What line?

BOY. That horizontal line? *(He pokes at her belly.)*

WOMAN. Don't! That was a crease, just a crease, from my pants or panties, I've been sitting! It's not a scar you freak!

BOY. It's all made up?

WOMAN. There is a Dr. Stevenson, but I don't really know him, otherwise, yes, it was all a story.

BOY. Why'd you tell it?

WOMAN. To stop your crying, to lighten the mood, we were just talking, Jesus, I was trying to make you feel better.

BOY. I feel worse.

WOMAN. The point I was trying to, the point, the moral of my story was, whether your mother, if she's dead or not, I don't care, it's just, come on, it's okay, you're not the first person that's gone through whatever it is you're going through.

BOY. Or the opposite.

WOMAN. Or the opposite, yeah … — Alice!

BOY. What?

WOMAN. Alice! *Through the Looking Glass*, Alice!

BOY. Alice.

WOMAN. Alice! Why was I thinking of Alice?

BOY. Because you drank the Bud which made you feel big, like Alice after she drank the "drink me" drink. And then you wanted to bite the Dorito, like Alice bit the "eat me" cake, so you could feel small again.

WOMAN. That's stupid, why would Alice want to be small?

BOY. Because she was too big to get through that teeny tiny door.

WOMAN. What door?

BOY. You wanna get out of here?

WOMAN. And go where?

BOY. I'll show you the answer to all your questions.

WOMAN. I don't have any questions.

BOY. Then I'll show you the question to all your answers. *(Boy leans in and kisses woman.)* Let's just walk. To stay warm. *(He goes. She sits.)*

Scene 4

Cemetery, several graves, the half-finished bag of Doritos on one.

WOMAN. *(Off.)* Robert! Hey! Hallooo! Robert! *(She enters carrying her remaining beer and bottle in a bag.)* Where are you, you little shit. I nearly just ripped my shitty coat on that shitty fence you just made me shitting hop. I don't hop fences Robert, I'm a lady! Worse yet I nearly broke my bottle! Not that there would've been much to lose in a breaking, as much or most of the contents are gone. But I coulda been cut! Plus the remainder beers are all shook up now. Gotta quarter tap 'em to keep from getting sprayed all over. And I don't have a quarter. Or a nickel or dime. And worse yet I'm freezing! And drunk! Thank god, or else I'd be worse freezing. "Worse freezing." Who says that? Drunk ladies in cemeteries chasing seventeen-year-old boys putting on lipstick in case they catch 'em, that's who. What're we doing, a little graveyard hide 'n' seek? *(She starts sneaking up and peeking behind headstones.)* Peek … a … boo! Peek … a … boo! Peek … a …

MAN. *(Off.)* Boo! *(Man emerges, ghostlike, from behind a grave.)*

WOMAN. Holy Jesus! Fuck you, fuck you, fuck you in the face, forever. That is bullshit!

MAN. What're you doing up here?

WOMAN. Jesus Christ, that was horrible. I nearly just threw up out of fright!

MAN. Why are you up here?

WOMAN. Jesus —

MAN. Are you chasing after my son?

WOMAN. What? No!

MAN. Because I could hear you screaming his name through the cemetery all the way down at my store. *(Beat.)* It's okay. I just figured I sold you a lot of booze, and it's cold, and if he ran off, which it looks like he did, you might get lost and hurt yourself.

WOMAN. I'm not drunk.

MAN. That bag looks lighter.

WOMAN. I'm not saying I haven't drunk … some beers … and whiskies. I'm saying the drinking of the drinks didn't make me drunk. Should I be worried about where your son's gotten to?

MAN. Most likely he saw me coming and hurried on home. Did you guys come up here to make out?

WOMAN. No! I'm old enough to be his —

MAN. You're older. I've seen your ID.

WOMAN. Har har har.

MAN. Got a flashlight. Need help getting outta here?

WOMAN. Why don't you have a beer and calm down?

MAN. You're asking me to have a drink with you?

WOMAN. Beggars can't be picky. *(Woman hands a beer to him. He opens it. It sprays him.)*

MAN. Motherfucker.

WOMAN. Oh my god! That's terrible! What kind of novelty joke shop are you running down there, selling exploding beer cans to the public?!

MAN. So if you didn't come up here to score with my son —

WOMAN. Vandalism.

MAN. Better.

WOMAN. Yeah, we came up to do some tagging. Tag a couple graves.

MAN. Where's your spray paint?

WOMAN. Hardware store was closed. You got a Sharpie? *(She fishes in her purse.)*

MAN. I don't think kids tag any more.

WOMAN. What do they do then?

MAN. They post. And tweet.

WOMAN. They call it what?

MAN. Actually, you can be tagged in a photo.

WOMAN. What?

MAN. On the internet?

WOMAN. My computer's at the mechanic. I'm talking about tagging. Outside.

MAN. My son's generation does its vandalism inside.

WOMAN. Your son's generation is sad.

MAN. They know. I read all about it on my son's Facebook page.

WOMAN. Oooo, look at you, modern man.

MAN. Why not charge a new laptop on that credit card?

WOMAN. That's right, mock the poor lady. No computer, no car, no dignity, no pen —

MAN. Probably no bra neither.

WOMAN. Ha! You're right! *(She flashes her breasts at him.)*

MAN. Whoa.

WOMAN. What? I already flashed my stomach tonight, compared to that the rest of my body's a ten.

MAN. You flashed my son your stomach?

WOMAN. He wanted to see my appendix scar.

MAN. Wait, so, you were gonna write your name —

WOMAN. Tag my tag name —

MAN. On a gravestone?

WOMAN. On as many as I can. Yeah.

MAN. Isn't that a little preemptive?

WOMAN. It's more a little fuck you.

MAN. To the deceased?

WOMAN. To the capital A Authorities. I just gotta think of a good tag name. I had this boyfriend in high school, your son and my's alma mater, straight edge kid, Benjamin Schuler, his tag name was TERD, T. E. R. D. It was so disgusting, and like the misspelling made no sense, it was an acronym, I can't remember the beginning, but the R and D were Random Destruction, maybe Rampant Destruction, Total Everywhere Random Destruction, so stupid. Because he could have spelled it T.U.R.D. right? With a U like for Utter, or Ultimate; but he was like, "I'm not writing T.U.R.D. all over the neighborhood, that would be gross." So it was Terrifying

Extra Random Destruction everywhere, on benches and doghouses and mailboxes; it was totally redundant in bathroom stalls. And then one night he just died in his sleep.

MAN. How old was he?

WOMAN. 28. He passed out drunk in his truck, drove into a lake.

MAN. So he drowned.

WOMAN. I like to think he fell asleep and never woke up. He's around here somewhere. My husband's just down the hill there. And then there's gotta be Mr. Quinn, or O'Keefe, and Matt Hoop, and all those other kids. Your son was telling me about all these kids. Wow, I can't remember ever talking so much about death in a night. I mean it makes sense. We all have it in common, like sports, or the weather. But, wow, there is so much, and we don't, y'know, talk about it. I mean do you mind? Talking about it? In a cemetery?

MAN. I don't mind. If there's beer. *(He takes another beer, quarter taps it, opens it, drinks.)*

WOMAN. It's, I find it relaxing.

MAN. TITS. That could be your tag name, T. I. T. S.

WOMAN. What does it stand for?

MAN. You have nice ones.

WOMAN. I like it. Ooooh, lipstick. *(She finds lipstick in her purse, she starts writing "TITS" tagger style, in lipstick on all the graves.)*

MAN. So, what were you doing in this neighborhood?

WOMAN. I had a checkup at the hospital.

MAN. Everything all right?

WOMAN. I'm clean.

MAN. That's good.

WOMAN. Friend where I used to work got me my old job back. Thanks, great, like I even asked. They needed the check-up to get me on their insurance before I start.

MAN. What's the job?

WOMAN. Real estate. Bullshit.

MAN. Gotta work.

WOMAN. Who says?

MAN They do.

WOMAN. Fuck them.

MAN. At least the checkup was good.

WOMAN. It was nothing, you fill out a form, they weigh you, take your blood pressure, temperature.

MAN. Quick though.

WOMAN. But, c'mon, run some tests, take some blood, something. Juice up the mammogram. Dig around a little.

MAN. Sometimes it's better not knowing.

WOMAN. No, but I mean, I'd been kind of getting my hopes up, y'know? When I got the appointment? There's no way I'm going back to that job, but that appointment. I mean I've got some symptoms, I've got no appetite, can't get out of bed.

MAN. Symptoms.

WOMAN. Symptoms, sure. So I got kind of hopeful. Crazier things have happened. It really got me out of bed, got me down to the doctor's. But then like, she's all done, and she's just a nurse practitioner, and I go, "So how's it look, doc, how long do you figure I got?" She looks at my chart, "Oh I'd say thirty, forty, maybe fifty years."

MAN. What does she know.

WOMAN. The fuck does she know, exactly, I could still be sick, she doesn't know. You didn't see a lump or anything? When I flashed you?

MAN. They looked healthy to me.

WOMAN. Perv.

MAN. Run into Mary?

WOMAN. Day off.

MAN. Lucky.

WOMAN. Sure, lucky for me, I didn't have to give her her card back and now I can keep charging groceries for the rest of my endless healthy life.

MAN. So, this is why you're out all night, trying to intoxicate my son and have your way with him in a graveyard?

WOMAN. Fuckin' A! I'd fuck you too, if I could just get drunk enough!

MAN. You're still gonna die eventually.

WOMAN. Yeah, that's not a huge fucking comfort.

MAN. Still pretty angry, huh?

WOMAN. You betcha.

MAN. That's cool. I'm good with anger.

WOMAN. Oh, you're good with it?

MAN. Yeah. Anger's a standalone for me. I don't think it's gotta be part of a process, a larger process. I think it can be its own thing ... Like negative feelings, anger, depression, what have you, they say they're always part of a process. Something that you go through to get to, I don't know, acceptance, right? So you can be happy again, right? But then positive feelings, like happiness or confidence, they don't have that stink on them, of just being part of a process. Of being something you should get over. People don't preach, "You should work through your happiness to get to acceptance that there's nothing to be happy about." Not that I'm against happiness. I just think it's hypocritical thinking. Let happiness be happiness, and let anger be anger, and don't tell my rage to run on your schedule. Man.

WOMAN. That must have been some divorce.

MAN. Yeah, right? I was speaking more generally, in a general way. Sorry, I got a little tipsy.

WOMAN. Tipsy?

MAN. Buzzed, whatever, a little buzzed.

WOMAN. On two beers? The Liquor Man's a light weight?

MAN. I didn't say drunk. But give me another; I'll get there. *(She flips him another beer, he quarter taps it, drinks.)* This the last one?

WOMAN. Your son drank the rest.

MAN. Me and my boy splitting a sixer. Warms you up, a cold beer. That's weird. Shit, it's cold.

WOMAN. Someone oughta make a run to the liquor store.

MAN. Ha. Yeah.

WOMAN. Really?

MAN. What? No. Come on, we can't stay out here all night, right? Eventually everyone's gonna have to pile in their cars and head home. Right?

WOMAN. Ugh. My car is like, the running joke of the night.

MAN. Then the bus, whatever.

WOMAN. I missed the bus. Literally. I keep missing the bus.

MAN. Well then you want a ride? I could drive you.

WOMAN. I don't know.

MAN. Why not?

WOMAN. You're kinda creepy.

MAN. A second ago you were ready to take advantage of me.

WOMAN. I was being charming. Now I'm feeling vulnerable, and I don't really feel comfortable riding in cars with strangers.

MAN. I'm not a stranger.

WOMAN. Do we know each other?

MAN. In a way.

WOMAN. See that's what I'm talking about, that's creepy.

MAN. I mean that we're not strangers in that that's my wife's grave you just vandalized.

WOMAN. Oh my god, I'm so sorry.

MAN. It's okay, you didn't know.

WOMAN. How could I? Stupid, stupid —

MAN. It's just a stone, I didn't mean to get sentimental, it's just —

WOMAN. I'm so, so sorry —

MAN. It's ok. It's good. I'd almost forgotten where this place was actually. It's been a while since I've been here.

WOMAN. I didn't know.

MAN. No, I'm sure. Just, just my kid being a wise ass. Leading you up here. *(Beat.)* I know my wife is, this isn't a surprise, y'know?

WOMAN. Okay.

MAN. I just didn't want to talk about it anymore at some point. Not that I have a lot of people to talk to.

WOMAN. Okay.

MAN. But you get sick of the pity party.

WOMAN. Yeah?

MAN. With divorce, it's disgusting, people don't ask follow-ups generally; try to make you feel better for fucking up a marriage.

WOMAN. Yeah.

MAN. They leave you alone.

WOMAN. Which is what you want.

MAN. Right.

WOMAN. Should I go?

MAN. Not yet. Unless you need to.

WOMAN. I don't need to.

MAN. Then do you mind staying just a little more? I haven't been up here for a while. It's a little scary.

WOMAN. Sure.

MAN. And this is nice. Opening up. With you.

WOMAN. I'm glad.

MAN. It's just when you have a kid you want to shield them from that, too. Having everyone feeling sorry for their dad, and for them.

WOMAN. I'm sure.

MAN. But then — You know, I had almost the exact same conversation with him about Santa Claus. One day, he's around five, he goes, "Was mommy real?" And I go, "Yes" and he goes, "Where is she?" and I — "She died," and he's, "Well then, where is she?" And there's no answer to that, unless you're religious, which I've always thought was the quitter's way out of using your head. But I try and

I say she left, she went "home," and he asks, "To the North Pole?" and he cries 'cuz it's so far, and you try to soothe, and you sort of bumble out, "No, closer — Long Island." And he's all, "What's it like, what's it like in Long Island?" And finally I say, "It's like heaven." And he's finally satisfied, so, so, so are you, finally.

WOMAN. Yeah, well, kids.

MAN. Of course, he figured it out, eventually, third grade, first time a kid from his school went to East Hampton for the summer, Robert couldn't believe he came back alive in the fall. So we talk it out again, but I still didn't have a better explanation than Long Island, so I stuck to it, like a mule, shrugging, going "Long Island, Long Island, Long Island." And then when he was in that crash with the kids, my son, and when he, when Robert didn't survive, that sealed it for me. I couldn't come up here anymore, with the two of them side by side, and me, no idea where they'd gone — *(He breaks down. She looks at the two graves of his wife and son.)* He didn't tell you? *(Silence.)* Makes sense. Who buys beer for a dead kid? *(She starts to go.)* Please don't go.

WOMAN. I have to ...

MAN. Please, I'm scared.

WOMAN. I can't stay. *(She walks off.)*

MAN. Don't go. You don't know what's out there. *(Pause, she returns.)* I'm sorry. *(Silence.)* I've never seen him. Since. I've tried running after him, out to the bus stop. I don't know. He probably knows I couldn't really take that. Seeing him. *(Silence.)* And what difference would it make anyway, right? *(Silence.)* But it's nice huh? How he takes care of me? Sending me visitors. And then sending a nice woman like you. Who gets it. To make me come up here? Get me to open up. It's nice. *(Pause.)* Are you all right?

WOMAN. No.

MAN. I'm sorry.

WOMAN. All right. *(Pause.)*

MAN. How, what was he like, Robert?

WOMAN. What?

MAN. How was he? What did he look like?

WOMAN. What did he look like?

MAN. Yeah.

WOMAN. He had on a hoodie and black jacket.

MAN. What else?

WOMAN. Jeans. Sneakers?

MAN. How did he seem?

WOMAN. I don't know.

MAN. Okay.

WOMAN. He talked a lot.

MAN. Oh yeah?

WOMAN. He wouldn't shut up.

MAN. What did he say?

WOMAN. I have no idea. He just talked, and talked, and talked. *(Pause.)*

MAN. What was your husband like?

WOMAN. I don't —

MAN All right.

WOMAN. It's all a little much, I'm still a little in shock I think …

MAN. Me too, always. It's like a state of perpetual fucking shock. *(She begins to weep.)* Oh come on.

WOMAN. I'm sorry.

MAN. No, I'm sorry, I'm sorry if this all was upsetting.

WOMAN. It was upsetting.

MAN. He looked like a nice man, your husband.

WOMAN. What?

MAN. From the store. The picture, you showed me his picture.

WOMAN. Oh my god. I thought —

MAN. *(Realizing.)* Oh, you thought, no, no, the picture, his picture, I know what he looks like from that, not from —

WOMAN. From him haunting your store —

MAN. Yeah, no, not that!

WOMAN. He's not walking around out there somewhere, drinking beers, asking after me —

MAN. No, no, not as far as I know. But who knows, y'know?

WOMAN. Right. *(Pause.)*

MAN. What happens now?

WOMAN. Now? *(Beat.)* Now, you should give me a ride, because I'm too sloppy and it's too freezing to wait on the bus.

MAN. Can I, could I give you my phone number?

WOMAN. Why would you do that?

MAN. I'm just asking if I could.

WOMAN. Sure, you could give me your number.

MAN. And maybe you'd call me sometime?

WOMAN. Sure, if my phone hasn't been disconnected.

MAN. What would we talk about, if you called?

WOMAN. I don't know, sports, the weather, movies. Anything.
MAN. Really?
WOMAN. Why not? We'd talk. We'd talk and talk and talk.
MAN. And that'd make things better? *(Beat.)* It's so cold.
WOMAN. So we should go. *(They don't move.)*

End of Play

PROPERTY LIST

$20 bill
Six-pack of Budweiser
Bottle of Jim Beam
Pack of Camel Lights
Sun Chips and Cool Ranch Doritos
Credit card and ID
Telephone and phone book
Tube of lipstick

SOUND EFFECTS

Bus arriving/departing